A Cornish Vision

150 Years of the Cornwall Blind Association

by John Clutterbuck

**Patron:
The Bishop of Truro,
The Right Reverend Bill Ind**

Subscribers
Mrs Gladys Carroll
Mrs Barbara Collier
Mrs Janet Bray
John and Lorna Hodgson
Mrs Tegwen Owen
Mr John Warner

Acknowledgments
Researched by: Judy Pryor, Gloria Alsey, John Clutterbuck, Dorothy Sweet.
Assisted with reading and summarising: Abi Preston, Lyn Preston, Nick Roberts, Jane Adams, Margaret Willis, Ethelwyn Parker, Nancy Tuffill, Richard Pryor, Geoff Fanner, Alison Jane, Kerry Keast.

Picture credits
Cornwall Studies Library, Redruth; Royal Cornwall Museum, Truro; Falmouth Arts Centre; Royal Pavilion, Libraries and Museums, Brighton & Hove; Omniglot.com (Simon Ager); The Sussex Lantern, Brighton; Halsgrove House, publishers; RNIB Archives, London (Clinton Lovell); Imperial War Museum, London; Kerry Keast; John Clutterbuck.
Front cover shows: A Cornish Miner; Lydia Smith; William Moon; CBA Chairman Martin Follett and Patron The Bishop of Truro.
Back cover shows: Frank Symons.

NB. Any opinions, errors or omissions are the responsibility of the author, not the CBA.
Published by Cornish World Media on behalf of the Cornwall Blind Association 2006.
Registered charity no 1108761.
Copyright Cornwall Blind Association ©

A catalogue record for this book is available from the British Library.
ISBN 0-9551069-1-5
Printed and bound in Cornwall by Headland Printers, Penzance.
Design and typesetting by Cornish World Media, Penzance.

All rights reserved. No part of this publication may be reproduced, stored in a retrieval system, or transmitted in any form or by any means, electronical, mechanical, photocopying, recording or otherwise without the prior permission of the Cornwall Blind Association.

Contents

Foreword by The Bishop of Truro — 6

Chapter One: Setting the Scene — 8

Chapter Two: The Formative Years - 1856-1918
    First Steps — 15
    The Teachers — 21
    Blind and Partially-Sighted People in Cornwall — 25
    The Finances — 29
    Social Work — 31
    Contemporary Activity — 32

Chapter Three: Mid-Life Crises - 1918-1970
    All Change — 35
    New Name, New Function — 40
    Rising Fortunes — 41
    Wartime — 45
    The Malabar Years — 46
    End of an Era — 49

Chapter Four: Bringing it up to Date 1970-2006
    Enter the Sight Centre — 52
    Came the Revolution — 56
    What's in a Name? — 58
    Looking Forward — 60

The Future: A Personal Reflection by CBA
Chief Executive Martin Pallett — 63

The Bishop of Truro
The Right Reverend Bill Ind
Lis Escop, Feock, Truro, Cornwall, TR3 6QQ
Tel: 01872 862657 Fax: 01872 862037
Email: bishop@truro.anglican.org

Foreword

Cornwall Blind Association is to be congratulated on producing this attractive and fascinating history of the association to commemorate the 150th anniversary of the association and its work.

Today, we see the ruins of engine houses dotted around parts of the Cornish countryside, but in the mid 19th century mining was active and widespread; it was hazardous too, for those that worked down the mines. Sadly, too many miners were blinded or suffered other serious injuries because of accidents, which were a frequent occurrence.

There was no NHS or social care systems in place to support those that were injured. Then, a new kind of embossed type became available, developed by a Brighton man called Moon, and soon a network of teachers of Moon started to support people across the Duchy. Here lay the foundations of today's Cornwall Blind Association, which has evolved and developed over the years and is now supporting more than 6,000 local people of all ages and backgrounds.

Visually-impaired people have a right to the same quality of life as anyone else and the association plays a major part in providing information, support and advice to blind and partially-sighted people in Cornwall.

The way that this support is delivered may have changed since the 1850s, but the underlying aim of the association – to support visually impaired people in improving their lives - has not changed to this day.

As patron, I have been impressed by the variety of ways in which this support is painstakingly given by staff and volunteers alike. I hope that this well-researched history will help everyone to realise the very real contribution that CBA continues to make now, in its 150th year.

The Bishop of Truro,
The Right Reverend Bill Ind

A Cornish Vision

150 Years of the Cornwall Blind Association

Setting the Scene

The Cornwall Blind Association is 150 years old in September 2006. It's changed its name two or three times along the way, and changed its main function several times too, but in essence it remains the only true local resource for visually-impaired people in the Duchy. In 1856, it was the first organised attempt to improve the lot of visually-impaired Cornish people, over a decade before the RNIB came into being.

In Cornwall at this time there was probably a greater chance of working men going blind than anywhere else in the country – because in the mid 19th century it was the most active mining district in the world. This is hard to believe in today's

> The 19th century was a pious age, and nearly all early attempts to help the visually-impaired were aimed above all at improving their spiritual well-being. Many different systems of raised or indented type had been developed, by which a poorly-sighted person could learn to read any of the scriptures that had been 'translated' into that particular type. Schools for the 'indigent' (that is, needy) blind were set up in various towns – there was one in Exeter from 1838 – but they catered primarily for visually-impaired children, or those who were blinded from birth. Those who had become blind in adult life weren't normally included.

Cornwall of scenic views and mass tourism; and the remains of engine houses dotted about the landscape give only a very small clue to the county's industrial past. It was all hard-rock mining, and the lodes of tin or copper had to be blasted out every inch of the way. Blasting was a hazardous occupation and there were frequent accidents, with many miners blinded – as well as

Dolcoath Mine Camborne, c.1890

maimed – by flying debris. There was no welfare scheme or insurance cover in those days of course, and blinded or crippled miners in Cornwall faced a bleak future. Those without private means often ended up begging by the roadside, or shut away in institutions that were little more than workhouses.

In 1845, a blind teacher in Brighton named William Moon devised a new kind of raised – or embossed – type, and began publishing 'translations' in a monthly magazine for visually-impaired people a couple of years later. The Moon system used a simplified form of normal lettering that was easy to learn, even for older people and those with limited feeling in their fingertips. William Moon began to promote his new type with missionary zeal, and it quickly became the most widely-used of the various raised-type methods. It's still in use today, as an alternative to Braille for those who have poor manual or mental dexterity.

Moon shifted the focus of teaching away from blind children towards blind adults and poorly-sighted. As it wasn't usually feasible for them to attend

> The first recorded use of incised type – ordinary letters carved on thin tablets of wood – was in 1517, and at least a dozen sorts of embossed type were circulating by the mid 1800s. Few of them were interchangeable, so they could only be used to read books specially translated into that particular type; in 1868, the Bible had already been produced in five different raised type systems. The Exeter Blind School, for instance, taught a system devised by a Mr Lucas of Bristol.

William Moon (left) and an example of his Moon type (above).

centralised schools, the idea of home teaching came to the fore (there had been some religious instruction 'at home' by The Indigent Blind Visiting Society in 1830s London, but this didn't include reading).

We don't know exactly when books in the Moon system were introduced into Cornwall, but it was probably before 1850. The Duchy wasn't entirely 'beyond the pale', and the local gentry kept abreast

> In 1855 the first official Home Teaching Society – in London – was started, by a committee of philanthropic people. They engaged a Moon-literate blind man, William Cooper, to seek out and teach visually-impaired people to read in their own homes, and supply them with 'translated' books (mainly scriptures) from a free lending library.

of new developments by travelling, receiving visitors and writing letters. Caroline Fox, the noted diarist (*Memories of Old Friends*, 1883), is one of the key figures of the time. She corresponded with William Moon, and is known to have tried teaching a blind girl to read The Lord's Prayer in raised stitches.

Caroline Fox, aged 27.

By 1852 or thereabouts, a blind man from St Austell, William Baker, had become such a good reader in Moon that he was employed by some local worthies to teach a few others and to start a library of embossed books in his district.

As it wasn't easy for people with sight loss to visit him, he went to them instead, and thus became the first unofficial 'home teacher' of visually-impaired people in Cornwall, and a vital element in the subsequent story of the Cornwall Blind Association.

The Society of Friends (Quakers), along with the Anglican clergy, and some of the more enlightened gentry in Cornwall, were doing what they could to improve conditions in the mines at this time, and the Royal Cornwall Polytechnic Society was one of their talking-shops. It was logical that the first steps towards creating a formal organisation for helping blinded miners in Cornwall should take place there.

The Formative Years – 1856-1918

First Steps

It wasn't really surprising that the Society which eventually became the Cornwall Blind Association was established in the mid-1850s. This was the very peak period of tin and copper mining in Cornwall, with over 400 active mines employing upwards of 20,000 miners above and below

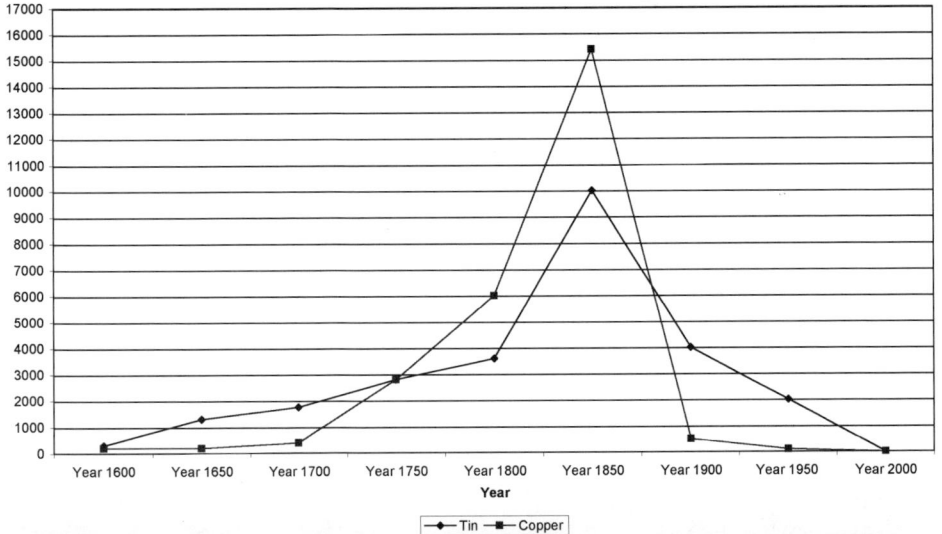

Copper and tin production in Cornwall.

ground. Conditions underground were harsh and accidents frequent. The need for almost daily blasting to progress the workings led to many injuries, and not infrequent blinding. Gunpowder (black powder) was still widely used, and the charge was usually detonated by applying a candle to the end of a straw filled with gunpowder. Even when detonators and safety fuses became the norm, accidents were caused by premature, delayed or mis-firing. Many blinded miners also

Conditions underground in a Cornish mine.

had other injuries as a result of the explosions, of course.

The Royal Cornwall Polytechnic Society (RCPS) had already promoted the development of the 'man-engine' for lifting miners to the surface after a shift, and better mine ventilation. In 1856 the time was ripe for another campaign. The Rev John Punnett, vicar of St Erth, was prominent in the RCPS. At the Annual Exhibition at Falmouth in September 1856 he gave an address explaining the need to set up an organisation to help the large number of blinded miners.

> The RCPS was founded in 1833 by Charles and Robert Fox – members of the same influential Quaker family as Caroline – to promote the arts and sciences. It's still in existence at Falmouth, though now merged with Falmouth Arts Centre. Aptly enough, in 1870 the RCPS Hall was severely damaged by a practical demonstration of a new explosive.

The Royal Cornwall Polytechnic Society.

The help he had in mind was essentially spiritual, to give them the chance to read the scriptures and other religious material, using embossed type. Gainful activities were also to be encouraged, of course, but had a distinctly secondary role.

The idea obviously struck a chord with his audience because, right after the meeting, a committee was set up to organise the Cornwall Home Teaching Society (the Society or CHTS). It was made up of Anglican vicars and Quakers – a fine example of ecumenical effort.

At first, a 'refuge' for the blind was suggested, where 'industrial arts' could be taught, with part of the expense offset by selling the items made. But it was eventually decided that, in the first year at least, a 'travelling agency' would be better; and as it turned out, teaching visually-impaired people by visiting them in their own homes was so successful that it was continued. In fact, the group was initially called the Society for the Itinerant

In his book, *Light for the Blind* (1873), William Moon wrote:

Cornwall

In this important county of mining operations an interesting work is being carried on, which was commenced at the same time as the one in London. In mining districts blindness is always more or less prevalent, owing to the accidents arising from the blasting of rocks and other causes.

A blind man, Mr Baker, was the first person employed to teach the miners and others who were blind in the neighbourhood of St Austell. Two teachers are now engaged for the county, who travel from place to place.

They remain for three months in places which they visit for the first time, and about one month at each subsequent visit, and instruct them in writing as well as reading. Great success has attended their labours.

The full list of the committee was:

Rev J Punnett,	Mr Charles Fox
	(Caroline's uncle)
Rev George Hadow	Mr John Allen
Rev E Tippett,	Mr T Coode
Rev JW Hawkesle,	Col Rose Winter
Rev Saltren Rogers	Mr William Hicks
Rev Charles Mann	Mr TB Bolitho
Rev JH Todd	Mr WM Tweedie*

*William Tweedie became Hon Treasurer, a position he kept for 42 years, until 1898.

Teaching of the Blind in the County of Cornwall (to read the sacred scriptures, and to write).

The Teachers

Blind or poorly-sighted men were thought the best to teach other blind men, presumably because they could empathise with their pupils; some of whom hadn't learned to read when sighted, of course.

Other injuries and the calluses on their hands made reading more difficult.

By 1856, William Baker had already been employed for four or five years to teach between eight and ten pupils to read the Scriptures, and with the help of his backers, he'd built up a small library of 'translated' books. Fortunately, Baker was willing to transfer his allegiance to the new Society, and became their first (and for the time being, sole) teacher at a wage of 15 shillings a week.

From St Austell, William Baker went to St Just, then to the Falmouth/Penryn district in December 1856 and the Truro district in April 1857. He also visited Liskeard and Redruth districts, but sadly died a short time later, in 1858, of 'congestion on the brain – not certified', aged just 42.

How did he (or any poorly-sighted teacher) find his way around? He must have had a guide, perhaps one of his children. It can't have been easy to move from district to district like that. Possibly the Society had a list of blind people in each district, and may have sent a scout to an area in advance to see who was willing to be taught - then worked out an itinerary for the teacher?

There's no record of who took over as teacher after William Baker. In fact, the Annual Reports of the Society before 1872 have been lost, and we only have snippets of information as reported in the Royal Cornwall Gazette, and the RCPS transactions.

A pupil of William Baker, a Tommy James of St Just – blinded and minus one arm from an explosion – was engaged by the Mission for the Teaching of the Blind to go to the gold-mining town of Ballarat, South Australia, where blinded miners (many of them Cornish) were even more numerous than at home. He taught blind people in Australia for 43 years, and one Harry S Prescott was inspired by him to start a Home Teaching Society in New South Wales in 1877.

Andrew Thomas became the home teacher in 1860; other early teachers were John Williams of St Just (perhaps a student of Baker's) who was appointed in 1865, and John Andrewartha. Both of these last two were also travelling insurance agents, which must have fitted in very well with their teaching duties. In 1897, there were two teachers; one of them, Richard Gatley, continued for the next 35 years, retiring in May 1933. In 1918, he is reported to have covered 11 districts, for 10 days to 7 weeks at a time, and made 680 visits.

An important part of the teachers' duties later on was to correspond (presumably by typing in Braille) with their pupils between visits, to give them some reading practice. But by 1916, the National Lending Library of embossed books had become free of charge; and with 27,000 titles to choose from, there was less need for this effort from the teachers.

Blind and Partially-Sighted People in Cornwall

An article in the Royal Cornwall Gazette, February 1863, estimated that there were then about 500 blind people then in the county. From that time

> William Moon wrote, in a letter to Caroline Fox (October 1856), about the practice in London:
>
> "The teachers set out in the morning for their particular portions of their district for the day, taking with them two to four books, in two bags slung across their shoulders. They make their first call and change the book, taking it to the next reader, and so shifting each book from one reader to another till they complete their round for the day. By this means, one set of books supplies a large number of readers and the books are conveyed from one to another without any difficulty. The teacher at each visit hears them read a little by way of improvement etc, at the same time having a little spiritual conversation and prayer with them."

until the start of the Great War, the numbers gradually declined, following the reduction in mining activity. A list of 'some 250' Cornish blind people were sent from a new Government register in 1918 (there's no mention of the 'partially-sighted' until much later on).

From 1897, there began to be records of miners blinded by explosions abroad, particularly in America and Africa. As the domestic mines closed, many Cornish miners went abroad to work; and

> Visually-impaired people didn't just sit around; they are recorded as working at basket and mat making; chair caning; needlework/knitting; massage (in one case); gardening; clock repairing; selling fruit, milk, eggs, sand and coal; farm work; piano tuning; concertina playing; and umbrella mending. In some areas, such as Calstock, many of them had 'tea agencies' and went out on regular rounds selling tea – which made it hard for the teacher to find them.
> *But how did they find their way about?*

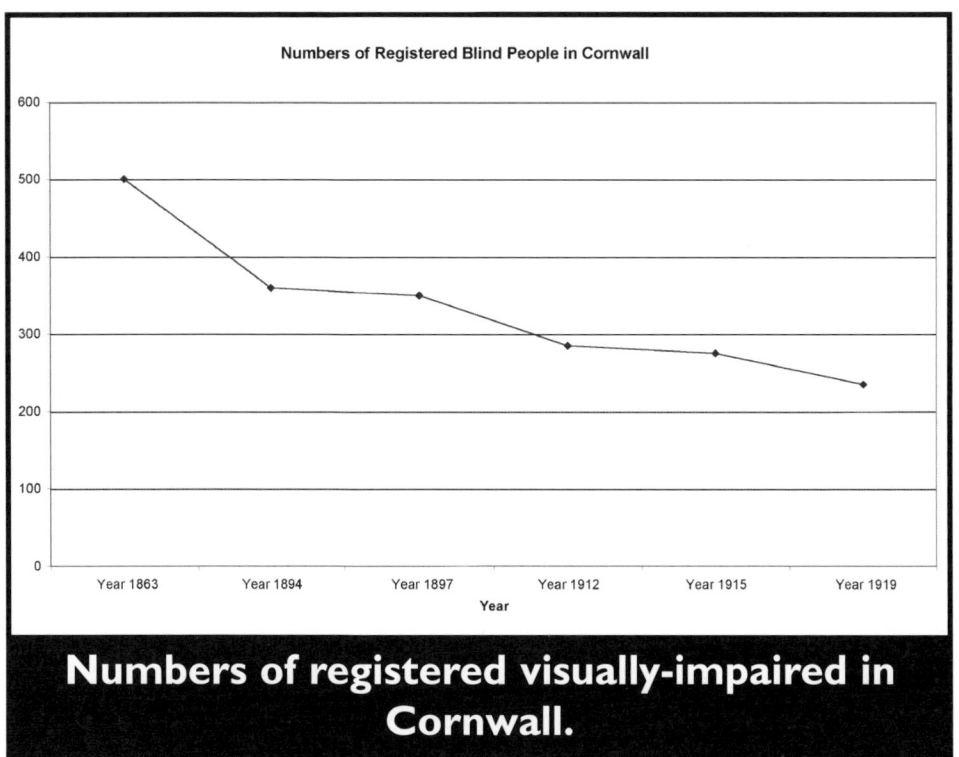

Numbers of registered visually-impaired in Cornwall.

some of them returned home blinded. "It is perhaps peculiar to Cornwall the number of people blinded in a mine abroad" was a comment in the 1898 Annual Report.

From 1899 onward, there were more reports of non-miners being taught – people blinded by farming accidents, through fits, from cataracts, from studying chemistry, from measles, from old age, from a blow on the head, from paralysis of

A visually-impaired typist at work.

The first British-made typewriter – the Hughes Typograph, patented in 1850 – was specifically designed to help visually-impaired people communicate with society at large (after all, a touch typist doesn't need to look at the keyboard). We don't know when these typewriters were first introduced in Cornwall, but they were certainly being provided by the Cornwall Home Teaching Society (CHTS) in 1890.

the nerves, or from glaucoma. During the Great War numbers must have begun to rise again because of reactivated mining operations and, of course, from active service.

The Finances

The Society paid the wages of the one or two teachers, contributed half of the cost of books bought by blind pupils, and funded small libraries of books (in Moon and Braille) in the various sub-districts. Eventually, typewriters were also made available, with the Society paying two-thirds of the cost (in 1890 a basic typewriter cost 17/6, a really good one a guinea).

The 1905-6 accounts show the scale of operations:

Income

Balance b/fwd	£ 15.15.10
Subscriptions & donations	£ 90. 4. 0
Books, papers etc donated	£ 2. 3. 7
Total income	£108. 3. 5

Outgoings

Wages & travelling expenses of teachers	£72. 5. 1
Books, papers, typewriters	£ 6. 0. 0
Donation to British & Foreign Blind Assoc	£ 1. 0. 0
Printing of Annual Report	£ 3. 0. 0
Cost of collecting subscriptions	£ 3. 3. 0
Postage & stamps	£ 0.16.10
Total outgoings	£86.04.11
Balance c/fwd	£21.18. 6

At first, acquaintances approached by the committee members subscribed to Society funds individually. But by 1910, collection of donations by volunteers had started, and this may be the first time that 'ordinary' people had become involved with the Society.

Social Work

Gradually, the Society took up a more social role. Teas and entertainments for the visually-impaired began to be organised on a regular basis. And in time, the teacher/s were expected to consider their pupils' financial needs, and not just their spiritual well-being.

They provided some training in the various craft activities like basket making, and advised about selling the products. In cases of particular need they could procure small one-off grants from the Society, and they arranged pensions for those who had none.

In 1911, a list of sources for blind persons' pensions was given:

244 from Heatherington's Charity
27 from Royal Blind Pension
6 from the Dowager Lady Robinson's fund*
13 from The Blind Man's Friend Charity
8 from the National Blind Relief Society
8 from the Cloth Workers Company
6 from the Gardeners Trust
5 from the Poor Adult Blind Society
3 from the Painter Stainers Company

* In 1895, £15,000 was bequeathed to set up the Dowager Lady Robinson's Fund for the Blind; investment interest to be paid to or for the benefit of the blind of Penzance, Redruth, Camborne & St Just districts.

Contemporary Activity

William Moon travelled widely during the late 1800s, and encouraged the establishment of a number of other home teaching societies using his system. By 1861, there were similar societies in

Bristol, Edinburgh, Birmingham, Liverpool and Bradford. In fact Moon became the only system to be used country-wide, until it was overtaken by Braille. There were other innovators. In 1860, for instance, the South Devon & Cornwall Institution

> It was in 1868 that wealthy London physician Dr Thomas Armitage, himself affected by of sight loss, became concerned about the large number of different embossed-type systems, and after much deliberation chose Braille as the best one for general use, reserving Moon for the elderly or horny-handed people. Braille was devised (by Frenchman Louis Braille) back in 1829, but as it uses a combination of six raised dots rather than trying to mimic conventional letters, it had been slow to catch on.
>
> Dr Armitage and his associates formed the British and Foreign Blind Association to promote Braille (and Moon); and this eventually became the National Institute for the Blind, adding 'Royal' in 1953 to become the familiar RNIB.

Reading Braille.

for (the Instruction and Employment of) the Blind opened a school in part of the old Plymouth workhouse. This organisation became closely linked to the Society in the 1920s.

In 1908, a number of regional bodies were set up, and Cornwall came under the umbrella of the Western Counties Association (originally 'Union') for the Blind. This didn't appear to affect the Society at the time, but became much more significant after the Great War, as we shall see (incidentally, the Devonport & Western Counties Association for the Blind, with its 'home for the unemployable blind' at Torr, near Plymouth, confusingly seems to have had nothing to do with the other Western Counties Association; it was founded in 1860).

Mid-Life Crises: 1918-1970

All Change

By 1918, the Society was at a low ebb. Incoming subscriptions were less than £100 a year – barely enough to fund the employment of two teachers, one full-time and one half-time. Blinded ex-soldiers were coming to (or back to) Cornwall, and another teacher was sorely needed – to help maintain the benefit of short reading courses provided by charities like St Dunstans. It was felt that the subscription list needed to be at least doubled, and an effort had to be made to make the Society better known.

A year later, everything had changed. In 1919, a Ministry of Health initiative for the visually-impaired began, which led to the Blind Persons Act, passed in 1920. All societies for people with sight loss now had to be registered and to co-operate with each

Blinded servicemen in the Great War.

other. Suddenly the Society became part of the Establishment, instead of just another independent provincial charity. The Society was made accountable to the Western Counties Association for the Blind, (the regional body set up in 1908) and had to send in monthly reports to headquarters. The committee was also expected to work in partnership with the Plymouth-based South Devon & Cornwall Institution and with the county council.

In return, Ministry of Health funding of up to £78 a year now became available for registered home teachers, provided always that the teaching led to employment and self-sufficiency; spiritual comfort was no longer enough. The county was to be divided into four regions, with a teacher in each – a doubling of the teaching staff at a stroke.

As a sign of this new co-operative climate, the two extra teachers needed were appointed, paid for,

A visually-impaired basket weaver.

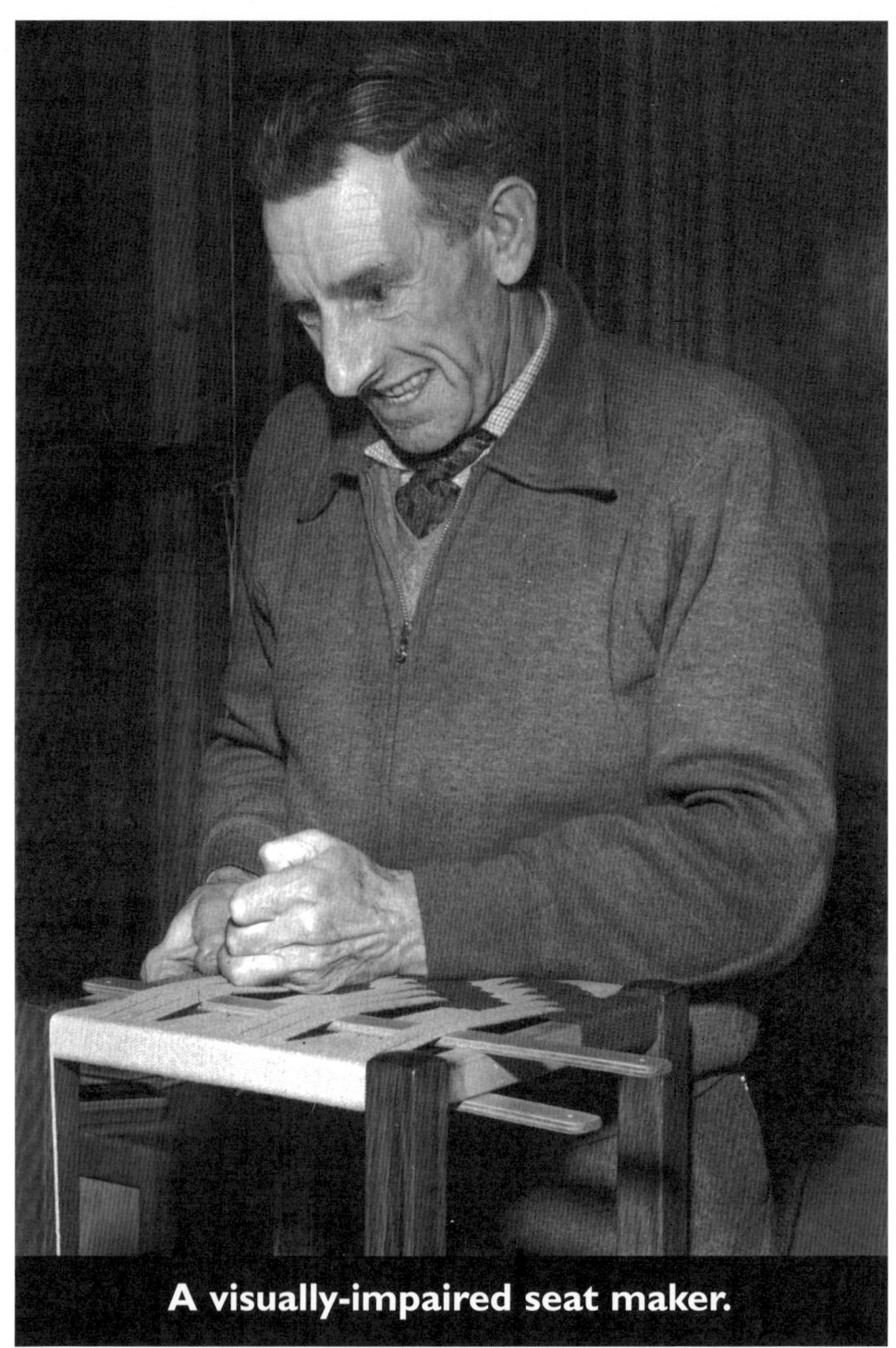

A visually-impaired seat maker.

and sent down to Cornwall by the London Home Teaching Society (later absorbed into the National Institute).

But it wasn't long before something went wrong. The two organisations fell out in a big way, and the new teachers were unceremoniously called back to London. The Annual Report for 1921 is vague about the cause of the dispute, but it wouldn't be surprising if the local committee resented outside 'interference' after being independent for so long. Perhaps as a direct result of this dispute, control of all the home teachers in Cornwall between 1923 and 1927 was transferred to the South Devon & Cornwall Institution (acting for Cornwall County Council). It was they who appointed, supervised and paid the teachers (through the Ministry grant of £78 per teacher), while the Society just contributed towards the travelling expenses of two teachers.

So what did the Home Teaching Society do without

any home teachers? The first thing was to change the name – to The Home Teaching Society of the Blind in Cornwall, and County Association with the South Devon & Cornwall Institution for the Blind. This must have seemed a good idea at the time, but thankfully it was shortened two years later (in 1925) to The Cornwall County Association for the Blind (the Association or CCAB) – and in the process lost all reference to home teaching.

New Name, New Function

During this time, the objectives of the Society-turned-Association also had to be redefined. Now its main functions were: to maintain the register of blind people in Cornwall; to recommend (to the county council) suitable pupils for elementary or adult schooling; and to arrange pensions from the state or from voluntary societies. In effect, there was a shift towards social administration. But the charitable aspects continued, and with the help of a team of volunteer collectors, subscriptions from within Cornwall were rising steadily.

Books and other aids for people living with sight loss were still distributed, although mechanical equipment such as typewriters were now lent rather than donated, with the blind recipient paying 2/6 or 5/- a year, and returning the equipment when it was no longer needed. Local sub-committees were formed to discuss needy cases, and small amounts of money were distributed for various things, with the assistance of grants from both the National Institute and the Western Counties Association.

Rising Fortunes

1927 was a good year for the Association. Voluntary collections in Cornwall became pooled, and far more funds suddenly became available. After many attempts to avoid overlapping collections, a scheme had finally been agreed whereby Cornwall – the CCAB – kept all subscriptions, legacies and donations received, plus three quarters of all money raised by public collections for the blind in Cornwall.

The remaining quarter was taken by the National Institute, as a contribution to sight loss services nationally.

From October of that year, the Association also took back control of the home teachers. By this time, most of the sighted teachers were preferred (not least because they could get around by themselves, of course), and there had been a definite shift towards employing women rather than men. One or two teachers now had their own cars, and the Association's increase in income meant that it was possible to buy an Austin 7 car for the use of another teacher.

The role of the home teachers themselves was changing, too. By this time most of the poorly-sighted people in the county were considered to be too old for lessons either in reading or in handicrafts, and the teachers spent a lot of their time simply arranging for, and distributing, pensions. From 1935, they were also responsible for distributing statutory financial assistance to 'the necessitous blind'.

The county was now divided into 5 districts, with a teacher in each. One of them, Miss Barker, became secretary of the Association and the 'supervisor of teachers' in 1930 – a post she held for the next 20 years. The number of visually-impaired people in Cornwall was now over 500 and rising.

The Austin Seven.

An annual outing to Newquay was instituted in the early 1930s, and at Christmas, more than a 100 Christmas hampers were sent out by the National Institute in Exeter and distributed by the home teachers. The teachers also began distributing free radios from the British Wireless for the Blind Fund.

Sales of poorly-sighted workers' products were organised, and a stall taken at the Royal Cornwall

Visually-impaired workers.

Show. In 1938 a shop window was taken in Truro to showcase some items, manned by volunteers. Eventually a part-time paid shop manager was appointed.

Wartime

The war brought more work for the home teachers, in difficult conditions. The blackout plus petrol and other shortages, all conspired against them, just at a time when the poorly-sighted population in Cornwall was being swelled by evacuees. Their salaries were eventually increased so for the first time, visually-impaired teachers received as much as fully-sighted ones, if they were fully qualified.

During the war, there were new attempts to address the social needs of the visually-impaired. In 1943, an institution was started which flourishes to this day – the monthly social, now known as the Blind Club. The very first one was held at Launceston, and the idea rapidly caught on elsewhere. Launceston was also the home of a team of hand-bell ringers in 1945, and a discussion group was started at Redruth.

The Malabar Years

By the time the war ended, more than half the visually-impaired population of Cornwall was aged over 70. The Association was in surprisingly good shape financially (mainly through increased donations), and it was decided the time was ripe to open a home for the infirm visually-impaired. Malabar House, a run-down Victorian mansion in Truro, was duly purchased for just over £7,000, and fitted out, essentially as a specialist nursing home for those (almost all elderly) people with

> Previously, elderly Cornish blind people whose family couldn't – or wouldn't – take them in had no refuge apart from the workhouse or the almshouse. There were some specialised nursing homes for the blind in other parts of the country, but they could scarcely supply enough beds for their own residents, let alone take in some from other areas.

sight loss who were no longer able to care for themselves, and had no-one else to look after them. It received its first residents in December 1948, and was declared officially open on February 18, 1949, by the Lord Lieutenant of Cornwall, Colonel Bolitho.

Malabar, the first 'home for the blind' in Cornwall, was a real milestone in the Association's history. Its day-to-day running presented a completely new set of challenges for what was still a non-professional body, and a separate sub-committee was set up to administer it. The project seems to have been a great success, with the home's capacity of 22 residents quickly reached. A new extension was built in 1954, named the Grenfell Block after the Treasurer of the previous 30 years – bringing the total number of beds to about 35.

For the first time, the Association had a permanent centre for its activities. Regular socials and handicraft sessions were started there, both for the residents and for others in the Truro area. An annual Malabar Rally was held for all Cornwall's visually-impaired; 300 attended in 1965.

Malabar House.

Gradually though, ideas changed. The National Health Service Act of 1948 promoted council-run residential homes for elderly people, which also began to take in visually-impaired residents; and it was quickly apparent that most elderly blind people with sight loss actually preferred to be with sighted people, and to stay in their local area. Only those who had been blind from an early age were happy to live just with other blind people. After less than 20 years, Malabar had become an anachronism.

In 1965, Malabar took in its first sighted person on a temporary basis, because of a shortage of beds elsewhere in the county. Permanent rooms for three sighted residents were prepared on the top floor, but – unsurprisingly perhaps – no sighted people really wanted to go there.

End of an Era

The National Health Service Act had also made local authorities responsible for employing home teachers. At the time though, Cornwall County Council had asked the Association to continue looking after them. But, by 1965, the role of home teachers was so weighted towards social welfare work that the committee decided it was time to let them go. On March 31, 1966, the county council finally took over the home teachers, renaming them 'social workers for the blind and visually-impaired', a function they still carry out today; and so more than a 100 years of tradition finally came to an end.

By this time, Malabar House had become an embarrassing financial burden. The committee was unhappy that a large proportion of the Association's time, energy and financial resources was being spent on just 35 of the nearly 1,000 blind and partially-sighted people in the county. As a result, in the early 1970s it was arranged that Malabar should be transferred to the county council and its status as a Home for the Blind ended.

The finances of the Association immediately improved. In place of a perpetual drain on resources, the sale of Malabar injected around £17,000 into the coffers. The house was maintained as a council-run home (for sighted as well as blind residents) for a number of years, before being sold off and converted into flats. The imposing Victorian façade of the main building remains virtually unaltered to this day.

With the departure of the home teachers, and the transfer of Malabar, the Association's remit for the social welfare of the visually-impaired also passed to the local authority, together with responsibility for maintaining the register.

It marked a new phase for the Association; a chance to reinvent itself as a body dedicated to helping the poorly-sighted people of Cornwall through the work of volunteers, using donated funds.

Bringing It Up To Date 1970-2006

Enter the Sight Centre

The sale of Malabar, no home teachers' salaries, and an increasing income from the sharing of donations with the RNIB, had boosted the Association's resources to around £75,000 by 1972. This healthy bank balance made it easier to upgrade facilities, and begin new projects. But without home teachers new ways to contact Cornwall's visually-impaired people had to be devised.

The obvious way of doing this was to harness the potential of local volunteers more. Through befriending schemes, help with transport, and through various activity clubs, the swelling army of volunteers became a crucial part of the Association in the 1970s, as it still is today.

Every army needs officers and a chain of command. The funds were now available to take on professional office staff, but, with the disposal of Malabar, the Association again had no permanent base. The first, temporary, solution was to rent office space in Truro with the Cornwall Rural Community Council (the CRCC), a non-profit body which provides logistical back-up to local charities.

The CRCC helped to fund the Association's first paid staff members – a director (later renamed general manager), assistant manager and secretary (but not a treasurer – that remained an honorary post until 1998). It was the first small step in the Association's sea-change into an efficient modern organisation; and there was no going back.

That first director, Gloria Alsey, set about raising the Association's profile. She cultivated the movers and shakers in Cornwall – the same level of society that had subscribed to its earliest development – as well as getting the general public involved through wacky fundraising events, such as a tandem ride from Liskeard to the Isle of Man, started by Chay Blyth. As a result, donations and legacies rose dramatically, to the extent that the fund-sharing agreement with the RNIB was discontinued. With this rising income, other ways to help visually-impaired people (VIPs) became possible, besides giving grants and organising local activities. The Association slowly began to take a more active role in providing specially-adapted tools and comforts for daily living, and it became clear that a permanent base for teaching and demonstrating these tools was going to be needed.

By the late 1980s assets of over £1 million had been built up, and it was time to make a move. After much discussion, Penryn House (part of the redevelopment on Newham Road, Truro) was purchased, and in mid-1994 the Sight Centre was opened. Now there was not only a place for 'service users' (in the new jargon) to learn new things, but also a meeting place for volunteers, trustees and committees, and adequate office space for the growing number of staff (totalling eight in 1995). There was even room for expansion, with one floor let out for the time being to Talking Newspapers and other tenants. Although Newham Road was never going to be an ideal

The Sight Centre, Truro.

location because of access and parking problems, it was indeed a giant step forward.

Came the Revolution

An influential group of visually-impaired people (VIPs) set up the Cornwall Blind Consultative Group (CBCG) in late 1994, essentially to monitor the Association's activities. At that time, as it had been since way back in 1856, virtually all the trustees were fully-sighted. The CBCG was the first to recognise that there was a need for greater VIP involvement in the organisation. Only blind and partially-sighted people really knew what was in their own best interests, so why shouldn't they have a bigger say in running *their* Association?

The 1996 annual general meeting (AGM) was the flash-point for revolution. The top floor of the Sight Centre was packed out, with an overflow of people on the stairs. Some harsh words were spoken against the sighted trustees, and accepting that confidence had been lost, they all resigned on the spot. VIPs took their place, and at one fell swoop the Association changed from a traditional grant-giving charity to a fully-fledged self-help organisation.

To help resolve conflicting agendas, the general committee spawned a number of separate sub-committees, with a steering group (comprising the director, chairman and treasurer) 'running the show' from day to day. With an organisation now equal in size to a medium-sized business, there were plenty of challenges to confront.

> As one might expect, the new trustees didn't always have an easy ride. They lacked the management skills and committee experience of the 'old guard', and often found themselves being pulled in different directions. In effect they were pioneers of the 'stakeholder' model of disabled help - as a partnership between professionals and service users - that is now at the core of official government policy.

What's in a Name?

From 1996, stimulated by an external consultant's report, the Association introduced a series of exciting new initiatives, many of which are a familiar part of its services today. The quarterly magazine Outlook was started, as a way to maintain links between volunteers, subscribers and users. The access technology section was formed

The first edition of Outlook.

(run by Alison Jane), as soon as the potential benefits of the new technology for people with sight loss became obvious. A basic website was set up, to make contact with the wider world. Contracts were gained from the National Health Service (NHS) for the provision of low-vision aids, and from Social Services for distributing talking books.

A qualified counsellor was retained to provide emotional support and a professional fund-raising team – led by Capt Gerry Jones, himself registered blind – was engaged, not just to bring in more cash, but to raise the Association's profile.

> Paying over £50,000 a year for professional fund-raising was always going to be controversial, and this particular arrangement survived for four years before it was dissolved with some acrimony. In those four years, the team brought in just over £300,000, at a cost of £217,000. The value of the publicity gained must have been substantial.

To go with the image make-over, there was a change of name in early 1997, mainly to get rid of the patronising tone implied in Cornwall County Association *for* the Blind, but partly also to avoid confusion between CCAB and CAB (the Citizen's Advice Bureau). So at last it became CBA – the now-familiar title of Cornwall Blind Association.

Looking Forward

A social services review in 2002 identified 3,447 visually impaired people in Cornwall who had received support. But this is probably just the tip of the iceberg – there are many more with serious sight difficulties, and registration of visual impairment is voluntary. It has been estimated that there may be upwards of 10,000 people with some sort of visual impairment in Cornwall now.

> One high-profile event around this time was a garden party at Trewithen House attended by Princess Anne, with the Lord Lieutenant of Cornwall and some 300 VIPs. It was an expensive 'do', but worthwhile for the resulting publicity.

Nationally, it's claimed that 90 per cent of people over 60 have some visual impairment. In Cornwall – with a large number of retirees, coupled with rural isolation and low incomes – it's an even bigger problem than elsewhere. There is a growing need for more training (especially in computer aids), more work opportunities, emotional support, advice about helpful services and products, and simply help with getting out and about. This is essentially what the CBA is there for. But many affected people in Cornwall still don't know of its existence, and there's a clear need to raise its profile even more. That's why future plans include organising major events, a better web presence, local fund-raising groups, and possibly even a community radio station.

For various reasons, the Association's income has not kept up with outgoings in recent years, so the reserves are gradually being eroded. More fund-raising, and increasing grant income, is therefore very high on the agenda – and this would also be helped by greater publicity. The possibility of moving to a more accessible building has been discussed, but for the present, the focus is on making the existing building more 'user-friendly'.

There are a number of other improvements and changes in the pipeline, but for the CBA's continued success, everything depends on keeping the Association in the public eye. The CBA has recently been converted to a public limited company, limiting the financial liability of the trustees, so that promotional projects can be a little more adventurous in future.

The CBA is now a modern non-profit organisation run on sound management principles; a far cry indeed from its distant origins 150 years ago as a Society for the Itinerant Teaching of the Blind to Read the Scriptures. But, in principle at least, its values are still the same – to help improve the lives (both physical and emotional) of all visually-impaired people in the Duchy of Cornwall.

The Future - A Personal Reflection

By Cornwall Blind Association (CBA) Chief Executive Martin Pallett

We have come a long way in the last ten years since we moved from a small office in River Street to the present Sight Centre premises in Newham Road, Truro. This previous office provided a central point for the Association to issue grants

Martin Pallett speaks with CBA clients.

and support a small number of clubs but it was felt that the establishment of a resource centre would enable many new services to be set up and developed including a Low Vision Service. For those who need more than a handheld magnifier, the Access Technology Service can provide a detailed assessment and advice about a range of electronic video magnifiers, (known also as closed-circuit television systems) and talking scanners, and specialist computer equipment. For those who need help with developing their computer skills, training classes are held in conjunction with the Workers' Educational Association. A specialist counselling service is also able to assist visually-impaired people too. Importantly the Association has over 300 volunteers supporting visually-impaired people as volunteer drivers, befrienders and at some of the CBA linked Clubs.

These and many more services are provided by a small dedicated staff team with the support of very many more volunteers. Inevitably with these developments, have had to come the necessary financial and administrative back-up that any small professional organisation requires.

What of the future?

New services will be required as funding and space allows. Already the new Benefits Take-up service and the Talking Support Service (2005) are meeting very significant needs as they continue to become better known. Befrienders already provide important support to visually-impaired people in their own homes but, with an ageing population and increasing awareness of isolation, more home support will be needed. Cornwall covers a large area and CBA will need to consider hard how it can begin to develop services across all parts of the county. This will require time, energy and commitment as well as funds.

The CBA has worked hard in the last few years to boost its profile. Still too many people either don't know that it exists or believe it is a branch of one of the big national charities. This is a major concern which is being addressed but requires sustained and continued attention. The CBA also needs to continue to broaden its appeal so that it is not just seen as an organisation of, and for, the blind. Very few people are what is termed 'black blind' and the CBA needs to provide the broadest umbrella and be prepared to work with any organisations and agencies committed to supporting people with sight difficulties however slight or severe these may be.

CBA clients enjoying a summer evening on the Carrick Roads.

It is important that blind people are involved in running and helping to steer the CBA forward for the future. As membership continues to grow, a foundation of visually-impaired people who are significant stakeholders of CBA and what it stands for, is a major strength which we need to nourish and develop. Important too, are financial resources. Traditionally the CBA finances have been regarded by other local charities with some envy but the Association has been a victim of its own success and income each year never quite matches expenditure. For income we have been too dependant on the National Health Service (NHS) and social services and we require a greater variety of funding sources. Legacy income has been very helpful in some years but fundraising needs to continue to develop. A top priority has to be to put the CBA finances on a more secure footing.

The CBA has to move with the times. It must not forget what it was set up to do – to support visually-impaired people but it needs to be seen as a modern pro-active organisation open to new ideas and constantly trying to improve and develop the support it provides to visually-impaired people of all ages.

We need to be both ambitious and realistic. Visually-impaired people have a right to so much more! Local campaigning by the CBA in recent years has been a constructive way of engaging with visually-impaired people and taking action to deal with the issues that affect them in their daily lives. This is an important area of work. To support visually-impaired people more we need to grow as an organisation and that means money, time and energy. With an ageing population and growing awareness, needs will grow.

Too many visually-impaired people need more support in their own homes and feel unable to take part in interests and activities that the rest of us take for granted. There are still many leisure time pursuits that visually-impaired people feel unable to pursue. There is a growing and developing interest in a whole range of blind sports.

There are visually-impaired people who have never worked and would love to be simply given a chance in the job market. There are people who cannot afford the specialist equipment they require to help them access basic information or

Blind at Sea (BATS) sailing club on the water.

communicate with others. Technology really does have the potential to improve the lives of visually-impaired people.

As it continually advances more equipment becomes available for blind people but often it is expensive and not necessarily within the reach of everyone who really needs it. There are huge training needs for blind people and despite disability legislation, too much discrimination taking place.

The CBA needs to grow to help tackle these issues but this will mean a rather different kind of genuinely county wide organisation will need to develop. This is really exciting but it will be tough and hard work.

We have a lot to be proud of in our 150th Anniversary year but there is still so much more we could be doing.